PRAISE FOR *TWO SIGNATURES*

"Internal severance certainly compels these staggering poems to the page, yet this book is no mirror. Sara Ellen Fowler's insight arrives from other worlds fraught with schism: Eros both fuses and flees. Art might guide or banish you. Some endings that hold were mistakes. Far from a book of despair, *Two Signatures* gathers wisdom from paradox, gathers in both body and mind a yes to the pained hope that 'One cannot be made whole the same way twice.'"

—**Katie Ford**, author of *If You Have to Go*

"In language carried on air, in the cellular material of generations, each poem in *Two Signatures* traces its source invisibly across the spine of another. The poems work inside the body with an explicit sensual, grave, and rare haunting. They settle inside first like a bridge from one life to the next but soon as a fractured web of one life to the many and the many to the impossible count. The poems piece back from their hard light the scattered, the unspooled, the untethered and the strange, taking incident and moment into a terrible, godly reunion."

—**Asher Hartman**, artist and theater maker

"The images and questions presented in *Two Signatures* will haunt you in the best way. Fowler is a genius at articulating the mysterious experience of being a body among other bodies—what it means to touch, to be touched, to be pulled apart by the world around us. These poems challenge the borders and boundaries of language, invoking moments of transcendence in vignettes of horses, fields, and lovers. This collection speaks in a voice both idiosyncratic and beautiful as we witness the interior landscapes of a curious and longing mind unfold before us."

—**Joshua Jennifer Espinoza**, author of *I Don't Want to Be Understood*

"Declaring to 'believe in the horizon only,' Sara Ellen Fowler in this extraordinary debut continually looks outward, looks at the spaces in between—the spaces both perceived and beyond our grasp. In stunning lyrics that are both eclogue and elegy, that are built from barrel races, FFA jackets, and brushfires leaping the lanes of freeway, Fowler engages a poetics of natural and supernatural means. But 'could language be altar enough'? Working in portraiture, in plein air, in ekphrasis, Fowler finds solace somewhere between the visual and the verbal, finds sustenance and beauty—poem after gorgeous poem—within attentive and exquisite forms where even the horse's hoof holds the 'private archive of their ride.'"

—**Brandon Som**, author of *Tripas*

"In *Two Signatures*, Sara Ellen Fowler writes a body-forward poetry, meaning its twin foci are its obligation to the bodies of words and its obligation to animal bodies, human and otherwise. It is a poetry that glorifies bodies honestly, as one hears in the music and attentiveness of lines like, 'tip toes up up to loop the belt to try to get their neck up to it,' and 'cat head on the lawn the impossible red the overcast red.' It is a poetry that doesn't settle for beauty, but aims for the sublime—it is a poetry that is Fowler's own, meaning, as is the case with all singular poetries, in it the world is seen for the first time."

—**Shane McCrae**, author of *The Many Hundreds of the Scent*

"Sara Ellen Fowler's debut collection, *Two Signatures*, sculpts a private language from the exquisite heat of longing and bewilderment. 'I am listening with my skin for her,' Fowler writes, and later commands, 'Hurt me / like this: let me // know your teeth as dearly as / I study my mother.' Allied with Dickinson's measure of knowing, Fowler's lyrics alter my temperature, like physical touch, culminating in a sensual decapitation. Yes, as Fowler writes, 'love has taken us down / word for word.' Yes, this book is a gift of intimacy and transformation made tangible in its reaching. An extraordinary debut—highly recommended."

—**Allison Benis White**, author of *Please Bury Me in This*

Two Signatures

THE AGHA SHAHID ALI PRIZE IN POETRY

TWO SIGNATURES

Sara Ellen Fowler

Foreword by Joan Naviyuk Kane

THE UNIVERSITY OF UTAH PRESS
Salt Lake City

AGHA SHAHID ALI

PRIZE IN POETRY

Copyright © 2024 by The University of Utah Press. All rights reserved.

The Defiance House Man colophon is a registered trademark
of the University of Utah Press. It is based on a four-foot-tall
Ancient Puebloan pictograph (late PIII) near Glen Canyon, Utah.

LIBRARY OF CONGRESS CATALOGING-IN-PUBLICATION DATA
Names: Fowler, Sara Ellen, author
Title: Two Signatures / Sara Ellen Fowler.
Description: Salt Lake City : University of Utah Press, [2024]

Identifiers: LCCN 2023055167
ISBN 9781647691868 (paperback : alk. paper)
ISBN 9781647691875 (ebk)

LC record available at https://lccn.loc.gov/2023055167

Errata and further information on this and other titles available at UofUpress.com
Printed and bound in the United States of America.

to my mother for my hands

and to B. R.

CONTENTS

FOREWORD

The poems in *Two Signatures* barbellate with lexical apperception. To read them aloud or on the page makes us aware that language—by which I mean diction—proves voice as much as it ratifies thought and choice. And Sara Ellen Fowler's precise, dynamic inflections remind me of a careful sentence in Barbara Johnson's introductory note to her 1987 volume *A World of Difference*: "Being positioned as a woman is not something that is entirely voluntary." I bring the citation of Barbara's words into and alongside the resplendent pages of *Two Signatures* not just because I found traces of Barbara—a woman whose theoretical teachings brought me to life (by which I mean literature) in ways no other could—in the poems you have before you, but also because these poems read and reread blind by me alongside the many strong manuscripts submitted for publication articulated the unforeseen crises and necessities of womanhood in the contemporary moment in ways that recursively amplify the deaths and lives of Sylvia Plath and Marni Ludwig. The former poet brought me into college and Barbara's classrooms; the latter poet, a classmate of mine in graduate school, helped get me out of classrooms and into the world. Note that the epigraph of Marni Ludwig's was not included in the original manuscript, and I found myself stunned at the uncanny coincidence of seeing the words of my dead peer as one of the epigraphs of *Two Signatures*. Now, that's too much about me, though hopefully enough to heighten and complexify the pleasure of reading *Two Signatures* for yourself.

As one of the early poems in *Two Signatures* declares: "I want to believe myself outside the art." May these poems restore belief, engender it. May their formal turns, episodic brilliances, and insistences make this dark time outside of art less so. Indeed, as a few lines in the poem "Blue-brown morning, I step through common starlings" breathe forth:

> There are only tracks and tracers.
> This is not home, I am not home, but this lea fixes me bold.
>
> There is a creature just beyond my sightline.
> I mark our lyric time unhanded.

—Joan Naviyuk Kane

You gave us each in secret something to perceive.

Franz Wright

I went swimming with horses.

Marni Ludwig

Good Mare

That I was
your simple bit

      a bride of pressure and prayer you ground
      grinding down

The one who taps your teeth to get you to open

—to be led be led
       let me in
          this psychic adumbration

      hitch a band of chances   the old tack chiming a hymn's cadence

Whose presence in the grain pail sweet   warm, warm enough, you bow your head
             and tug the leather lead in whose hands—

      eternal cipher under tongue metallic rub
      by the snaggy corners of your mouth

         I, your simple bit

I did not abandon you
when the barn burned with contempt

     I slipped from the hayloft
—your whinnies, cinders, the vicious air—

             I screened your eyes
              with a wet scarf
                to guide you through
                  the falling rafters

one

WARNING STARS

Glassell Park

There is no casual relationship.
Strung taut
            looping load looping adamant I see
    a soul
               at the Chevron on Verdugo

    Someone already no one reaches toward
    already omitted

                           One who's made their own shroud

in front of the topiary
at the Chevron and the rush-hour intersection fifty yards wide

One invisible twilit forgotten

Soul draped in a bedsheet
inked with scriptures of innermost math
      spiraling ordinations
               in ballpoint pen and permanent marker and pencil

under the crosswalk sign belt in hand
wavers a slow ascension attempts to string up to strangle

               I am a holy fool
           and can't stop looking
    remembering

         I don't understand
         galldread fucking wonder I remember:

         Another life
            My neck
            in a horse barn
            with no shoes on

Soul grapples with cut eye holes calling in night
            and the influence of their private divinity inching
tip toes up up to loop the belt to try to get their neck up to it

            Belt biting belt biting the shroud the skin

                        A horse barn,
                        my neck. Because my neck

        homes my voice
        remembers

        everything that happened and how

                                    ended for me last time

                                    with no shoes on

                        others there   and watching

I did not ask if it was my turn.
I did not ask what would become of my body.

I will not tell you what I said to my own self then.

But I ask that you use your teeth, please touch,
please, let me

remember the yellow bones of air inside the taking—

kiss the throat of my fate
with shut eyes
breath held down
kiss the throat of my last fate

Could language be altar enough

      in front of the topiary
      at the Chevron on Verdugo

            Saint and Martyr, Soul, in this world I am so sorry
I did not reach toward you

did not stop or call anyone

The Cutters

for *my teacher*

I see your face in the whetstone of mine

˵

You might misremember my dress in rain, light moving across it satin
as though any raphe seam could cry intercession

˵

The private lessons of unbecoming, please please

into anything anything else

˵

I just want to learn, to be admitted.
I want to believe myself outside the art.

And you reach under your ribs with a knife
just a little hook of pain, you curve
no testament no abstraction

˵

shiv of quiet

˵

Big seed, little star—
cat head on the lawn the impossible red the overcast red

I do not comprehend the current traveling

up my arm until she spooks
and throws her head away
      from my touch.

I'd leaned on the electric fence separating the paddocks
exactly as I reached for her muzzle.

          I register the broken faith   her rejection
          first
          then the fire
in my nerves.
        I am so primed to be

the wet foal abandoned in a cold spring field
no tongue to clean me up.

Window

The horizon measures itself in stillness. The fennel's coming through in the dark. Linseed oil carries on the draft from the unscreened window, west-facing little message of trust. My canvases fain shudder in the temperature like a horse's rippling will. I believe in the horizon only. O, let me be hulled in it. A mixed pulse, a wash of, I take the pills: silent dress circle of what care I need to keep painting here. The coffee's ready. And my lonelinesses fess no milk but patience. For the white-throated swift will call across the sagebrush. I am listening with my skin for her. Were it my steady line gathering definition in the morning purple grey, and gratitude its own prism, we could sit the hour and watch the light break the face of the high desert.

Lithium

I was but
        a young, unlearned water diviner—
the stick in my hand

toward my heart badly bent.

Portrait with water

Something invisiblepink   Scalding metallic water I am not pulling my arms away
a belief system wrists rainbowed raw   an altar an altar of attention

          I sit down to write the same word again and again with a scratch pen
dipped in Sumi ink

                    until I don't recognize my own hand until
the language too slips into a second legibility

                         reading to gesture and negative space the inner the outer
kerning waving

          learn the fabric learn the pattern
                              until I draw something I don't understand

          watercolor watercolor watercolor watercolor
          watercolor watercolor watercolor watercolor watercolor watercolor
          watercolor water give give give give give give give give give
                    give give give give give give give give

          What feeling? A stunner of a king-hit hope—
                    that I touch the color with my cold breath
                    and that breath's a ballast.

                    Could it be full-feeling?
          How could I know. How could you know.

Velvet

In sun, my skin's transparencies cast

as if threadbare
cotton underwear, once,
                              bone-in sun,
once-white
knife.

Old Paint

The pasture levitates with weeds in a cold mist. The gelding draws the perimeter with mud-packed hooves. I keep my eyes low, quietly working the barbed wire spurs in my hands: warning stars with tufts of hair corona'd around them since 1988. And the FFA jacket abandoned in the barn adjourns into a nest of mice. Thou set this good corner. I come by with apples, emboss my palms with kinwishes, seal my prayer for egress upon the old paint's searching lips. His teeth smack a cipher so simple I've been overthinking it this whole life.

two

STILL LIFE

Painted monument in the night of my body

My spinal column
Made not of petals
   painted: "Hidcote pink" nor "Evelyn" nor "Rosette with rain coming through it."

How's this sun so bald, so vivid turnt
In the flowerface—

Not shimmering, no. Blood-gloam
Tender inside my hunger.

My sex
Made not of graphene
   painted: "Water with no life" nor "Bronze throatlight in the register of trust."

     I say, rather,
     It's the color of the feeling
     Of catching God.

Reading with Temperature

There are no tenets save for pressure: two pubic bones locked in friction
or sandstone or deadlines. Reading
                                    is wind
born of the uneven heating of the atmosphere by sun.

I pray for the entropy that will pull you apart with the most precision.

Lidless, lawless, air
                        the most intimate material
takes a wet braid and rends what, thick, falls around your throat.

You wash my face in your hands,
                                    rubbing your hands until they are hot,
you wash my face in your hands.

One cannot pray to the horses

when they are blasted apart with sun, with singing.
As if one could white-out appetite with weather and galloping,

could paint a stolen weapon
red with insect wings crushed in snow—we are pure

and maple-headed, frilling leaves
too bitter to eat too brittle to build with.

The last rites of the angels just harvest and burning, just melody
with two voices skating across disaster.   Lovers twin nothing
lest lust and oblivion.

You come for me

And spread my knees. The pit bull
must have been a bitch

—first to step toward jeopardy. Her latent heat coils
a holy capacity: her jaw—her lunge, seize, drag.

       But I'm not made like her.
I'm made in your image. My blood

only tastes like jeopardy. But it's nothing.
The bitch is the saint in the room

where we work out the formal feeling.
       And consent is but a hinge

          necked ardent.
             Some panting, white musk, until

my breath is just a hole. Hurt me
       like this: let me

know your teeth as dearly as
I study my mother.

Engram

A black lacquered table and a split black ribbon. In the face of the void,

bank on my flint cunt. There is no temperature like ours.

Black bow and the scissors used to curl it under. You are the exhale

before another sip of ether. Rutilant stones and flat water.

The subtle weather collects light like baby teeth,

traces a foreknown fire

up your will to my voice. There is no temperature like ours.

Untitled (daemon)

A daemon unlaced in the fuck,
      our lonelinesses
           the foam
                of a misremembered fever's name.
              Dark tonic
              understood to be care.

Black licorice

                  I'll never understand your mouthfeel
save for the long syllable of the freeway and sun-warmed books and
a deeper tense of god.

              How do you like what you have?

Brushfire jumps
five-lanes and rushes a brittle embankment.

Make a gesture with your hands about being inside my body. *Up & in.*
Bright trust laughing hope hope—what I wanted.

              Like that.

                            To get inside, to come,
                            to seize requires deliberate grace

of bone. Our coordination of hungers
first off—what I wanted.

Taste smoke through the sugar, and rife with what longing
blackened trees have inside them. *Again. Show me.*
Your black tongue.

Valentine,

you got your fingers from my body. The lining that would home an embryo has insisted through towel and smeared pillow. Trap music. Some flowers. I don't want to set my hair on fire, like yesterday. Inside the fuck it's like paint by numbers and clean bedclothes surrender to bloody fingers. We whir something beyond mirth. Pleasing you a rainbow cast in spit and circles. How we step toward the afternoon storm and launder everything in what was once-ice, once-ocean.

Night Shirt

Tell me how it feels to wear my night shirt
in the sun of her affections and how she warms
your skin to pricking. Tell me why
the rust chipped under her septum ring tastes
like a fluid bond.

Tell me the women sound like animals
as they are breaking through their bodies
and it is the most natural thing. What weather
is not drawn not heavenly. So high she
shatters into still life: bowl of ice, black
trash bag, camera, gag. Dearly sick
                              sundrop, make of me
a chartered thing and my shutter
just a stint of joy. I must know what you did
to her. Tell me with your eyes why we can't
go on this way.

Aloud

I'm tired
of air rent
in the name of sex.   I just want to read
to myself
and rest the words
in my mouth   a new temperature   altogether.

Garnet

Our missives inhumed for all time
beneath the king clone spiral:

> I remember the way you looked at me.

> Whatever whatever unconditionally.

Divination was so simple when we used our boring hands.
Our mouths would labor other transport—
bloodlight up from sand.

What I mean by temperature

The black jade necklace strung with gold flown
to the gate of my collarbones—
just a slice, a mouth of night
there—I trust
your weight suspended on my skin, a button pressed to open a small portal.

three

A LOOSE EXTENSION
OF AN EARLIER MEANING

I learn   to lick your spit off a pane of mirrored glass
and spit again,
grateful.

        My seizing
throat and watering mouth,   my desire to please, my desire
to be seen:

prill gift
for you,
my teacher.

        The crush
        tacks   with lust until my breath   is a gauze
        of asking for it.

Lightproof and no fingerprints.   No email thread. Kind of blessed—
yes, dip   and   bow   and   dismember.
I have no eyes,   I have only a mouth.

                                    ``

I learn

tension.
Turned
          as a flank of marble—
fingered veins, precise, how to cut in, you
made the chisel and its sheath, you
handed it to me,
                    my first instrument
of writing.
               I score and score the memory,
the backs of our hands
brushing
                    a sculpture
                    in a present tense who
                    does not seek closure.

                         ``

Because I am skulled with the thought of black snow & Mayfair's parking lot
spring trash melt where whoever found a hundred, white veins of rock salt
spider my pant legs.

I comb the icy asphalt
and no one bides dusk, watches
through the windshield, windchill zero.
The air textured with the fractal frost of waiting.

How I've loved is not how I meant to love.
Another Hot Hands packet I crush in my mouth.

,,

I learn to prepare

the ground.

Sandpapering elbow wrist wrist   circles insist the seams of gesso
melt a finish, a conjured skrim.

Prepare prepare. Devotion

is a loused thing worked this supple—

see how the light rests, so dearly its needles

leave a welcomed mark on the virgin's
wit:
        green gloss of an eager lyric
        with all the caesura left in it.

Teach me   teach me.
                                To be a nervy lay.   To stay, to stay,

                                ``

stay the gun and tawn-amber under glass the cloud coming down

adipocere a morning I understood a color unspoken

what husk all the good thinking about power

horse hair plaster magnetic field whisper under

the projection screen when my teacher gasped and came

the cover of self smoke night sand

a chord wrung out with a numb left side a little rain

at first grey coal depths and a silver gelatin portrait

was it a nascent shadow no sun through fretwork

my wet book throws light like language

holds-host ignition heals traction
                                    traction

``

Just give me a job like
a mask with no eyeholes, all the better to destroy my art with.

I seek the private things:
gessoed panels left to dry in a room with just one set of keys.

The set threaded into a birch branch in 1988, and now I could not cut them down
if I wanted to. They've grown inseparable. I mean time, what texture, is involution.
    I don't know what art is.
                Show me the ratty, loose-toothed key in your thigh.

``

A postcard, the modern bull shark jaw with its blue shadow
on a blue ground but
to the scale of my own jaw
What a smile—
Have I swallowed enough—
      My will is my own water

＂

four

OLD BOND

My mother was a barrel racer

Her thighs kept her on that horse
She whistled and sent Caesar flying across the corral
They could spin on a dime, singing
      Everybody proud, and Fredericktown was in a dry county, so it was just
pop and popcorn on raisers made of straw

                I wanted blood in the saddle
             Every ritual I took very seriously
           I couldn't kick my shadow hard enough to canter
              A stain to mean I was a woman

On the poet's thirtieth birthday, 1962

the blessing curve of the mare's throat latch
the poet's hair blown out of her white ribbon

Off the lunge,
her spiraling lessons

give way to
crop and sprint and

foam and song—
    to be known to be alone

Over Ariel's cannon and pastern I run my palms to silk.
Lift one hoof as though to kiss. I use the pick
to reach the private archive of their ride. Pick
the soil around the mare's frog, that tender, nervy Y.
Devon's meadow flowers embossed in each sole
—yellow letterforms—

Plath sang of pressure and of letting go

She held on she held on for dear life / her life dear in her
shaking thighs *release my fear*
release my life

Reading Plath

I take the severed ficus root in both my hands cradle the dense germ

to forgive the material
               suicidality
                    in each of our eras

    hold it faceted   still   faceted a wholeness
                                      bloodquiet
    and inside her leave-taking unanswerable I

smell the early mold in paper fibers not yet pulped even
not yet sodden nor determined to
       get it under our nails

     little book of

                 honor
                 what
                        was cut down kneeling
                 before
                 ether and enervation and a goodwill fucked
                 unaccompanied

                  I answer her with fig ink adamant and

                 some exquisite drive
                 to be prone

                      old bond

Light's loose skin

The relief of sitting in a dark room with others

while the spirit film murmurs rich loam.

A poor face rises, looking back into the negative space of a secret: Mirrors
are just water,

specified. To make a new likeness, new likeness. Crumpled t-shirts strewn around.
And depression
               is the cold polishing of a lens.

           The camera eats the true flame, forgets your name. Star-starved
           I climb columns of shadow and drink invisible, leaching water.

Right After, 1969

for Eva Hesse (1936-1970)

After anesthesia.

The head
opened.

After zero, after zed. After breakfast, after sleep, after song.

The lightning field. After plastics.

After Mother, fisticuffs, waltz.

Lift your arms, fused quartz.
The sunbeam collared in longing.
The registration of shadows upon drywall.

Fishing line   glimmers   taut   from ceiling to   S-S-S
wire hangers   turned to hooks with pliers   every line begins
with S.
               Slip.
         Sense refraction. Surface air. Seconds quiet. Signal processing. Sex.
               Slit open the open.
                           The salt;
                                 the stitches;
                                       the sanctuary.

                           An ordinary hunger.

As it is above, so bestow translucence.

As for the edge of tears,

desirousness.

As for ordination, radiance.

Elegy for Skip Lanz (1939-2021)

in Fredericktown, Ohio
  home of the FFA jacket

a thousand worksheet pages

photocopied from saddle-stitched workbooks   flower patterns   birds and sun

When you can no longer decide between two crayon colors, you wind the house key and TV remote into a talisman with packing tape. You walk a quarter mile down the road, get as far as Bobby's. You want to go live with the Amish, you will tell the officer. You don't carry your name with you when you go.

Rest

       wings toward the grey daze
right above the tree line.   Rest cannot

dodge the many minds sharp in air,
cannot sound, cannot envelop

the lowest register of sky.
               And I lie

beside you. I have the water.
I know

what depth charge is
strapped to the board you wield when you

descend to dreaming.
            I pray its wire loop will not hold.

Nightjar

Marni, Your whole *Pinwheel* is on the Internet.
Fucked breathwork can be a source of time travel.

Cast out into the weather of your blood, a fortune of grief.

Nightjar, Marni, where-all you are, I hope rest has swollen to bless you.
Smoking's breathwork, you'd never say.

Your weather-vane made a circuit
of a lightning herald—language white-lit ragged

an annihilated temperature. And I was a dog
searching for temperature.

A list of comforts. One. Softness was only
Mike Kelley soft: those stuffed toys.
Solitude marveled into alienation into art. Elevation, no trust.

Two. Someone in your cohort gave you an imperfect pack of cigarettes.

In the photograph, you are searching eyes and a pursing exhale.
In my clairaudience, the exhale has a vowel sound
—the umbilical fear rush that died when you died.

Do we carry our friendships into the ground with us?
Do they marvel too long in the sun
like mud-red-green cut stems of roses wrapped in cellophane?

I cast your weather-vane for a quiet altar.
You stayed up all night while your horses slept in their fly-masks.

Dear Marni, when you lift the roof of your mouth
when you let the air go, you make a cathedral of the letting go.

five

RECEIVER

Chicken

Under wing shadows in parking lots we fell, happy. Went looking for deep greens in paintings. Heart boundaries were chicken skin. That power hardly looked like power. Flatten down another healing dream, so mottled, so dog-eared, and answer questions with the whites of your eyes. So trance. Not wet in any sense! Want to eat something flamelike in an overcast room and sweat a little and maybe talk? Forget landscapes of air, asphalt, animals. Make tonic after rushed sex. Turmeric, pepper, honey. Milk, heat. Cook out some water, some weather. Unwashed, unspiritual guild of us.

Mare and all

Friend or mare.
Form and land.
Pray the form
till rivering end.

Praise the trail,
turn back when
the cedar casts its light
un-hemmed.

Mare and host and bough and fiend—cairns lost—

we go unseen.

I don't give a fuck you can't sing. Rancheras, Nirvana—alive to things.

Fault and form piques the filly's blood,
wings the night unborn.
                    You know I could.

Whole

I live for the curve of time my work is not
having been made but

                       being worked

   for love.

I don't know how to handle the precautions.

Inside the respirator my ego becomes vapor
endlessly inhaled. I can't read.

My own breath turns to sweat.
Across this faceclose pane I don't love anyone.

But glass filaments. But lengths of fiber—
A friendship spreads between my hands.

           One cannot be made whole the same way twice.

Snowblink

Home me in
the feathering breath above the radiator, the plate glass window.

Midnight lake beyond it
unlit snow falls into silver water falls
one state into another.

        My mind ferries me to the private museum.

I will my self this
silknear script, the handed penknife and

silence holds here about my neck.
             Gallery of
                    I pray you never
                    bracing

        have to say goodbye
     in the ripped-out way   in the eternal loop
            of water winter   snow archive   strata

                I love you   strata

        withstands

              the elements up-heaven.

Alone and beneath the lakedrunk buckling floor.

Mercy, afterimage.

To know the museum's specific air on my face   yes   rock salt   waterbird
oil paint

    asleep and thrusting.

Heave, Lake Michigan.

   `

I go to the museum and then I want to do something.

Like accelerate on black ice   in my mind.
Like gun a tree or glass thing. Abscond.

Underbody
endgrain
remember
how.

Bracelet for Who I Was

Dusk-blushed desert *shirt*
thrown over the *duct*
fastened still
by the weight of shone *stones*
sewn into inside *cuffs.*
Just a prayer to notch
gravity's buss. I had to
apply my hands to something
kind and my own and understood
to be dross.

Bezel for my mind

In the portrait, your subject was grace and my subject was grace.

How I remember you
is how you painted me. Observed in profile.
The slab of my face: reds, purples.
Green whispers in the eye socket.
I understand the palette was meant to be grace.
    But my eyes, milky with Lithium.
But the slowfolds of my salted brain starved the compass.
       And where did I go?
I traversed a dissolve, feeling as though my mind abandoned me. For a new vessel,
perhaps a seashell, perhaps a warm, woven basket made by my mother.
    But you painted my skin deftly in the flat light reflected off an empty bookshelf,
my hand on a desk like an oath.

How I remember you is how you painted your subject with no eyelashes, compassion's arrow missing the cowering hide.
I quivered. You clutched my likeness
in oil. And where my blue shirt met its first button: a fleur-de-lis of throat skin, thin
light and shadow.
    No bezel for my mind but the hours of you painting me. I watched the afternoon rake along the back of your easel, without music.

Texture

The silk-edged woven baby blanket—I used to suck the silk—
then it tore and twisted,
and in the back seat
of the minivan
driving across Ohio, Indiana, Illinois, Wisconsin
how I'd unknot the tangles
in the dark
with the reverence of a jeweler
blessing a neglected chain, you kept me safe,
fray poem of childhood.

Ars Poetica

So I use my middle name—the other woman
who holds me the day I am born.
NICU nurse whose counterpractice to soothing
premature infants
is singing harmony
into incandescent fields of drying oil paintings.
Three pounds, ten ounces shivering petals.
Shitting light, moment to moment,
purple: we triplets curl together on a blanket
in our in-utero constellation,
make a window into Mom's unlit body.
A neonatal hymn is a prayer with all vowels.
Ellen's countless daughters
chant an up-breathing chord.
I am the alto with the flashing maw.

Blue-brown morning, I step through common starlings

flushed from the field chirring one wit iced in air.
The bronze sun invites itself into winter's folding.

No one is looking for me
lit this revving way. And what kind of light, what *kind*?

> One to shatter volume into wings—
> that seems meant for my mind—
> calls time, ignition, beckons: look, look—
> the grain-glint needles the meadow snow and—

> My love, I found your hair tie in my jacket pocket.

There are only tracks and tracers.
This is not home, I am not home, but this lea fixes me bold.

There is a creature just beyond my sightline.
I mark our lyric time unhanded.

Receiver

an epithalamium

Light for light maybe blessed

        love has taken us down
word for word
                opening
                our ringing bodies—
           pulsing sun-sky
      ordains you
rascal of wind
        and I am
clear enough to fuck through

                    Name for name
                      we release
                          our signatures
                                like horses failing their bits

Parachute

Paper craft of wings assembling inside
a chrysalis and wrecked with starting over.

The new body shuddering and turning, turning,
not *toward*   except to say further
                         inside, fold, fold
an armature for flight.

This is one prayer. And

there were many workups and rehearsals, blasts
straining with extreme temperature and thrust. Until

you used the length of my body to measure and
tuck, quilt and press the kit to thirty-three pounds. Quietly.

Could have been jeweler's cloth, puckered silk. A furl
of wills—

      come back, come back.

            Drogue heart, air and light—

            I am waiting,
                looking up.

NOTES

"Window" is dedicated to the painter Agnes Martin and where she worked in Taos, New Mexico.

"Engram." An engram (noun) is a hypothetical permanent change in the brain accounting for the existence of memory; a memory trace.

"Black licorice." The question *How do you like what you have?* is attributed to Gertrude Stein, something she used to say at parties. An anecdote from Eileen Myles.

"Garnet." An anthill garnet is a gemstone found around the margins of anthills in Arizona that were excavated as the ants constructed their underground passages.

"[Because I am skulled with the thought]." The italicized language is   borrowed from the Carl Phillips poem, "Wherefore Less Lonely," published in *Pale Colors in a Tall Field*, 2020.

"Light's loose skin." The phrase "mirrors are just water specified" is derived from a project of Francesca Woodman's titled "Some Disordered Interior Geometries," 1981.

"*Right After*, 1969" and "Whole" are poems speaking to the life and sculpture of Eva Hesse.

"Nightjar" is dedicated to the poet Marni Ludwig.

"Snowblink." The Milwaukee Art Museum is one portal to the private museum.

"Bracelet for Who I Was" describes a sculpture installed by the author at ArtCenter College of Design in 2010.

"Bezel for my mind" cites a portrait painted by Èowyn Wilcox McComb in 2013.

ACKNOWLEDGMENTS

The poet wishes to thank the following publications where this work has been
  homed: *Interim*, *Gigantic Sequins*, and *Cream City Review*.
My family, my teachers, my peers, and close friends—thank you for the gift of
  your attention, advocacy, and love.
Most especially to my parents, my siblings, and my sweetheart, Bala.
To my UC Riverside colleagues and mentors—to make and be made in your
  company is my great good fortune. Thank you, Soleil, Ryan, Sarah, Carlina,
  Jen, Rax, Crystal, Pat, Roda, Gennyvera, Vic, Emily, and Miguel.
To the clot and to my dear community of poets and artists in Los Angeles—
  thank you for inspiring me to see this work to fruition.
Jack, Laurelin, Cindy, Jane, Meharban, Brody, Stephanie, Gillian, David, Cat,
  Mylo, Nate, Fleurette, and Gretchen—thank you for being my confidants and
  champions.
I would like to express deep gratitude for the guidance of my teachers—Allison
  Benis White, Katie Ford, Allison Adelle Hedge Coke, Brandon Som, Morgan
  Parker, Kim Young, and Kelly Frederick Mizer.